GW01403160

Original title:
Love's Blueprint

Copyright © 2024 Swan Charm
All rights reserved.

Author: Johan Kirsipuu
ISBN HARDBACK: 978-9916-89-325-8
ISBN PAPERBACK: 978-9916-89-326-5
ISBN EBOOK: 978-9916-89-327-2

The Design of Desire

In shadows deep, dreams spark and flare,
Yearning hearts, a fight laid bare.
Patterns twist, a fate divine,
In every glance, love's secret line.

Threads of hope weave through the night,
Longing shines, the stars ignite.
Sketching paths where hearts align,
The design of desire, so intertwined.

Tapestry of Emotions

Colors dance in vibrant hues,
Laughter mingles with silent blues.
Each thread tells a story bright,
In the weave, life finds its light.

Joy and sorrow blend and sway,
Woven memories day by day.
Through every tear, through every cheer,
A tapestry of emotions, crystal clear.

Whispers in the Blueprints

Lines and curves on paper laid,
Blueprints whisper, dreams portrayed.
In drafts of future, hope takes form,
A silent promise, calm in storm.

Hidden echoes call from deep,
Secrets shared, the mind can keep.
In every sketch, a chance to grow,
Whispers guide where lovers go.

The Canvas of Connection

A canvas stretched with vibrant care,
Brushstrokes mingle, hearts laid bare.
Colors blend, and moments gleam,
Connections forge in every dream.

With each layer, stories unfold,
In quiet touch, a warmth to hold.
Artistry in every breath,
The canvas of connection, life from death.

Beneath the Surface

In silence deep, the waters flow,
Secrets dancing, soft and low.
Beneath the waves, where shadows play,
Whispers linger, night and day.

Echoes of dreams in twilight's glow,
Lingering where the currents go.
With every tide, the stories weave,
Beneath the surface, hearts believe.

A hidden world, so vast, so wide,
Where hope and fear in stillness bide.
Tides of time, they pull and sway,
In the depths, lost words stay.

A tranquil depths, serene and clear,
In the silence, love draws near.
When all feels lost, and shadows creep,
Beneath the surface, secrets keep.

The Dance of Affection

In gentle sway, we take the floor,
With every step, we long for more.
The softest sigh, a tender glance,
We lose ourselves in sweet romance.

Around we twirl, in blissful grace,
Joy ignites with each embrace.
Laughter floats like fragrant air,
In this dance, we lay our cares.

The world fades out, we're lost in time,
Every heartbeat settles in rhyme.
With every turn, a promise made,
In the dance, our fears allayed.

As music swells, we shed our doubts,
In the rhythm, love shouts out.
Connected souls in perfect beat,
Together, whole, we feel complete.

Cadence of Companionship

In quiet hours, we share our thoughts,
Through laughter light and trials fought.
Side by side, a steady hand,
Together, faced, we take a stand.

Voices blend like softest song,
In perfect harmony, we belong.
Through storms and calm, our spirits rise,
In each other's gaze, the world complies.

A journey forged, both near and far,
In every moment, who we are.
Footsteps echo, paths entwined,
In our hearts, we always find.

With every breath, a bond we share,
In the cadence, life laid bare.
Companions true, forever bold,
In tales of warmth, our story told.

The Harmony of Heartstrings

In softest tones, the heartstrings play,
A melody that guides the way.
With every whisper, dreams ignite,
In harmony, we find our light.

Each note a bridge from me to you,
In every rhythm, love shines through.
Tuned to stories written in time,
Together we create a rhyme.

In laughter's echo, our spirits soar,
Harmony weaves forevermore.
Through ups and downs, we stay in tune,
In the silence, we can swoon.

The universe in every chord,
A love that needs no spoken word.
As heartstrings play, we dance along,
In this life, we sing our song.

Common Ground

In fields where shadows play,
We gather blooms of light,
A tapestry we lay,
Threads binding day and night.

With every step we tread,
Paths converge in embrace,
Whispers softly spread,
In this shared, sacred space.

Hearts echo in rhythm,
Find the strength to stand,
Built on quiet wisdom,
Together, hand in hand.

Bridges span the divide,
Crafted from trust and care,
In unity, we bide,
Finding solace there.

So let us weave our dreams,
In colors vast and bright,
For in this dance of themes,
We find our shared light.

The Weave of Intimacy

Threads of laughter intertwine,
Stitched through every glance,
Moments soft and divine,
In the dance of our chance.

Whispers in the night air,
Secrets shared so sweet,
Holding onto our care,
At the heart, we meet.

Each conversation flows,
Like rivers, deep and wide,
Binding what we expose,
With nothing left to hide.

Embracing the quiet,
Finding peace in the calm,
In the shade we sit,
Finding warmth in the balm.

Time is a gentle thread,
Weaving us ever tight,
In every word we've said,
Crafting love's pure light.

Cartography of Togetherness

Maps sketched in our minds,
Across the stars we travel,
Navigating heart and finds,
Where the bonds unravel.

Each moment a new star,
Marked by laughter's glow,
In distances afar,
We let our spirits flow.

With every step we stride,
The compass guides our way,
Holding love inside,
As night turns into day.

Exploring every peak,
Each valley has its song,
Through the words we speak,
In the right, we belong.

So let our journey chart,
A story yet untold,
In the map of the heart,
Together, bold and bold.

The Forge of Feelings

In the heat of the flame,
Our spirits start to bend,
Crafting moments that claim,
The love that we defend.

With every strike, we mold,
The metal of our dreams,
In patterns fierce and bold,
Shape what together seems.

The anvil's steady beat,
Echoes through the night,
In the rhythm of heat,
We find our shared light.

Through trials, we will grow,
Tempered in the fire,
Learning what we know,
Fusing heart's desire.

So let us craft with care,
In this forge, unite,
For in our love we share,
We shape the perfect light.

Navigating Infinity

In the vastness we search,
For stars lost in night's veil.
Each flicker a whisper,
In cosmic tales that prevail.

Guided by dreams afloat,
We trace the paths of light.
With courage as our sail,
We journey through the night.

Galaxies spin and dance,
In the fabric of our souls.
We weave our hearts in trance,
As time endlessly unfolds.

Waves of thought crash ashore,
Echoes of what could be.
In every heartbeat's lore,
Lies the pulse of the sea.

Together let us soar,
Beyond the bounds of time.
In this infinite dance,
We'll find our perfect rhyme.

The Essence of Us

In every glance exchanged,
A universe ignites.
The warmth of shared laughter,
Reaches far into nights.

With every breath we take,
We weave a silent bond.
Two souls intertwined tight,
In the depth of a pond.

The whispers of the heart,
In harmony they sing.
An echo of our dreams,
In the joy that we bring.

Together we can build,
A haven in the storm.
With hands held side by side,
In love, we find our form.

Through all the highs and lows,
Our essence ever grows.
In this dance of our lives,
The heart's truth always shows.

The Art of Together

With each brushstroke we share,
A canvas wide awaits.
In colors bold and bright,
We shape our fated fates.

Every laugh a bright hue,
Each tear a shade of gold.
Together we create,
A story yet untold.

Paths and dreams intertwine,
As we gather our might.
In the space between us,
Live our hopes, pure and bright.

The art of being us,
Is painted day by day.
In moments small and grand,
We find our perfect way.

With each masterpiece made,
We celebrate our trust.
In the gallery of hearts,
Lives the art of us.

Canvas of Comradeship

Strokes of laughter ring clear,
On this canvas we draw.
In the palette of friendship,
We challenge every flaw.

With colors pooled around,
Our spirits rise and glow.
Each story shared in joy,
In vibrant shades they flow.

Here in this sacred space,
Where hearts and dreams collide.
We build our sturdy bond,
In the warmth of our stride.

Through trials we stand firm,
Our colors blend as one.
With every shared moment,
A masterpiece begun.

In the gallery of life,
Our comradeship does bloom.
On this canvas we write,
A journey to consume.

Echoes of Enchantment

In the twilight, whispers dance,
Colors merge, a fleeting glance.
Moonlight weaves its silver thread,
Softly calling, dreams widespread.

Ancient trees in shadows sway,
Mystic songs guide hearts to play.
Under stars, the spirits hum,
Echoes deep, to which we come.

Waves of time, a gentle tide,
In the night where secrets bide.
Nature's heart, a lullaby,
Carried forth on breezes high.

In stillness, magic finds its way,
Enchanting night, transforming day.
Each moment holds a thousand tales,
In the echoes, the wonder prevails.

With every breath, we seek to find,
The hidden paths that intertwine.
Echoes of the past resound,
In the silence, love is found.

Navigating the Heart

In a world where dreams collide,
Hearts like ships on turning tide.
Waves of hope, the storms we brave,
Navigating love, the soul's own wave.

Charting courses through the dark,
Finding solace in a spark.
With every heartbeat, maps unfold,
Guiding us through tales untold.

Landmarks marked by laughter's grace,
Guiding stars in endless space.
Every journey leads us near,
To the places we hold dear.

Through the valleys and the peaks,
Every silence softly speaks.
In the compass of our fate,
Love's true north will never wait.

With each heartbeat, we embark,
Into the realms where dreams can spark.
Navigating paths of art,
Finding home within the heart.

The Serenity of Sync

In the rhythm of the day,
Harmony finds its own way.
Time and stillness intertwine,
In each moment, pure design.

Like the waves upon the shore,
Seamless dance forevermore.
Each heartbeat sings a gentle tune,
In the hush, we're lost in June.

Gentle breezes, whispers flow,
Softly guiding where we go.
In the twilight, shadows blend,
Serenity, our steadfast friend.

Every glance, a perfect beat,
In each silence, hearts repeat.
Connected souls, so intertwined,
In the sync, true peace we find.

Unity in every breath,
In the cycle, life and death.
Together, we will softly sink,
Into the depths of serene sync.

Foundations of Forever

Upon the ground where dreams are laid,
A tapestry of love displayed.
Every stone, a story told,
Foundations strong, unyielding, bold.

In this garden, hope can grow,
Roots entwined, together flow.
Nurtured by the sun's warm light,
Guiding us through day and night.

Weathered trails, we choose to walk,
In the silence, hear the talk.
Memories carved in time and space,
Forever imprinted, a warm embrace.

Through storms that may come and go,
Together, we stand strong, we know.
Hand in hand, side by side,
In each heartbeat, love's a guide.

Built on trust, on dreams we weave,
Foundations deep, we won't deceive.
As we grow, our roots run free,
In these bonds, our destiny.

The Architecture of Affection

In the quiet of the night,
We build castles made of dreams.
With each heartbeat, a new light,
Soft whispers, love's gentle themes.

Brick by brick, we lay our trust,
Foundations forged in tender sighs.
Every moment, gold's but dust,
Yet in your gaze, the stars arise.

Windows wide to endless skies,
Our laughter echoes, strong and free.
In this home where love never lies,
Together, just you and me.

Roofed with hopes and painted bright,
The seasons dance with grace and flow.
Through every storm, we hold on tight,
In this shelter, love will grow.

Walls adorned with memories sweet,
Time, like a river, flows unbent.
Anchored hearts, in leap and beat,
This architecture, our consent.

Crafting Our Togetherness

With hands of care, we mold the clay,
Each moment, sculpted side by side.
In laughter's warmth, we find our way,
In quiet hours, our hearts abide.

Threads of gold and silver weave,
The fabric of our shared embrace.
In every stitch, we dare believe,
That love creates the perfect space.

As colors blend in perfect hue,
Our dreams take flight, hands intertwined.
In this tapestry, a vision grew,
Together, fate is redefined.

With each sunset, shadows grow long,
Yet in the dusk, we find our song.
In whispers soft, the world feels strong,
In us, the right will always belong.

Crafted moments, time's caress,
In every smile, a sweet reply.
Together, we shall navigate this mess,
With love's compass, we reach the sky.

Whispers of Kindred Spirits

In the hush of twilight's glow,
We share secrets, heart to heart.
Connected souls that surely know,
In soft whispers, we won't part.

Every glance, a story shared,
Silent laughter, a gentle tease.
In this bond, we feel prepared,
To roam the world, just like the breeze.

Kindred spirits, hand in hand,
Bound by threads unseen and bright.
Together, we forever stand,
In shadows deep, we find our light.

Echos of love in the breeze,
Guided by stars that light the way.
In the quiet, hearts find ease,
In every moment, come what may.

Through the seasons, we shall dance,
In harmony, our spirits sing.
With every chance, a wild romance,
In whispers, we find everything.

Designs of Devotion

With careful strokes, the picture's framed,
Each line a promise, softly penned.
In devotion's art, we are named,
Together, through the trails we wend.

Colors splash on canvassed dreams,
Brushes dance with rhythm sweet.
In every trace, our heartbeat gleams,
In every touch, our lives complete.

Crafted faces, love's embrace,
Shapes entwined in endless grace.
With each design, we trace our space,
In devotion's warmth, we find our place.

Layers deep, the stories told,
In motions fluid, hand in hand.
In this masterpiece, we grow bold,
In every stroke, love's strong command.

Framed in time, we'll never part,
In every corner, memories store.
In devotion's realm, we share our heart,
Hand in hand, forevermore.

Pillars of Passion

In the glow of evening's light,
We gather dreams in heart's embrace,
With whispered hopes, and futures bright,
We chase the stars, our destined place.

Through trials faced and joys we share,
Each heartbeat echoes, strong and true,
A bond that's woven, beyond compare,
In every moment, just me and you.

With every touch, a spark ignites,
As flames of fervor rise and fall,
Together we'll conquer stormy nights,
Our passion, the anchor through it all.

In silence shared, our spirits meld,
A sacred trust that knows no bounds,
In laughter's dance, our love is held,
In harmony, our heartbeats sound.

The world may sway, yet we stand tall,
Pillars of passion, steadfast and grand,
Together we rise, together we fall,
Our fates entwined, hand in hand.

Elements of Enchantment

In moonlit nights, our dreams take flight,
With whispers soft, and magic spun,
The stars align to guide our sight,
In this world of wonder, we've just begun.

With every breath, the wind does sing,
Of stories shared and laughter's grace,
We dance beneath the clouds as they bring,
A tapestry of time, a warm embrace.

The earth beneath our feet feels true,
With roots that intertwine and grow,
A garden of hopes, painted in hue,
Where love's sweet fragrance ever flows.

From fire's glow, our passions spark,
The warmth ignites a blaze divine,
In every moment, we leave our mark,
With every heartbeat intertwined.

In every glance, a spell is cast,
Elements of enchantment, hearts aligned,
Together we weave a magic vast,
In this realm of wonder, forever entwined.

Crafting Connections

In the quiet moments, we find a thread,
Woven through laughter, tears, and light,
With every word that softly is said,
We craft connections, pure and bright.

Through shared adventures, our stories blend,
With every chapter, a deeper bond,
In all we face, we will not bend,
For together, we forge beyond.

With patience strong, and faith in place,
We build a bridge from heart to heart,
In every challenge, we find our grace,
In crafting connections, love's true art.

The canvas of life, where moments paint,
A masterpiece of every hue,
In imperfections, we find no faint,
For in our flaws, we find what's true.

Through all seasons, hand in hand,
Crafting connections that never sever,
In unity, we forever stand,
A love that blossoms, now and ever.

The Geometry of Togetherness

In angles sharp and curves that sway,
We find the patterns of our dreams,
Each figure formed in love's ballet,
In the geometry of togetherness, it seems.

Lines drawn close, yet freely roam,
In this space, we're never apart,
With every step, we build a home,
In the blueprint of the heart.

From points of light to shadows cast,
We map the contours of our fate,
In every moment, we hold steadfast,
In unity, we celebrate.

The formulas of laughter rise,
In symmetry, our souls unite,
With every glance, we realize,
In togetherness, we find our light.

Through circles drawn, we measure time,
In the geometry of love, we thrive,
Each angle sharp, yet so sublime,
Together forever, we come alive.

Portraits of Partnership

In the light, we find our grace,
Every smile a warm embrace.
Through the storms and quiet nights,
Together, we reach higher heights.

Hand in hand, we write our tale,
Hearts united, we will not fail.
In the laughter and the tears,
We paint our dreams throughout the years.

A canvas filled with vibrant hues,
In every color, love renews.
With every brush, we intertwine,
A masterpiece that's yours and mine.

Moments simple, moments grand,
Through every phase, we understand.
With open hearts, we learn and grow,
A shared journey, ever aglow.

Together, we take on the world,
With our sails, a love unfurled.
Two souls bound by trust and time,
In unity, we always shine.

An Atlas of Affection

This map we chart, with love as our guide,
In every corner, you're by my side.
From mountains high to rivers wide,
In every journey, we'll abide.

With every star, we softly dream,
In twilight's glow, our hearts will beam.
Across the currents, we will flow,
In this atlas of love we know.

Each landmark holds a memory bright,
As we travel through day and night.
With hands entwined, we from the start,
Mapped out forever, heart to heart.

In every season, we navigate,
Through winding paths, we celebrate.
With laughter echoing through the air,
An atlas guiding love so rare.

As mountains shift and rivers change,
In our togetherness, we'll arrange.
With endless love to light our way,
An atlas of affection, come what may.

A Voyage Together

Upon this sea, our vessel sways,
In harmony, we find our ways.
With every wave, we share the thrill,
Together, we shall brave the chill.

The horizon calls with whispers sweet,
In every heartbeat, our souls meet.
With sails unfurled, we chase the sun,
In this voyage, we are one.

Through storms that roar and skies so clear,
I hold you close, you have no fear.
With stars above to guide our fate,
We navigate love, never late.

From distant shores to hidden bays,
In every moment, love conveys.
Adventures shared, our spirits soar,
In unity, we'll seek for more.

A compass true, our hearts align,
In every journey, you are mine.
Together, we will rise and fall,
In this voyage, we give our all.

The Spirit of Us

Amidst the chaos, we find peace,
In quiet moments, love won't cease.
The spirit of us, a gentle song,
In harmony, we both belong.

Through trials faced and battles won,
We hold each other, two as one.
In whispered dreams and twilight gleams,
Together, we weave our golden dreams.

The laughter shared, the tender touch,
In every glance, we feel so much.
With every heartbeat, the spirit flows,
In every story, our love grows.

In life's embrace, we rise and bend,
With open arms, we shall transcend.
With passion fierce, we light the dark,
In every moment, we leave a mark.

The spirit of us, a flame so bright,
In stillness or in wild delight.
Together, forever, hand in hand,
In the spirit of us, we take our stand.

Vows Woven in Time

In whispers soft, we carved our names,
Threads of love igniting flames.
Promises wrapped in twilight's glow,
Together, we'll face what winds may blow.

With every heartbeat, vows declared,
Moments cherished, souls laid bare.
Through seasons' change, we'll stand as one,
In woven dreams, our journey begun.

Time moves swift, but we're entwined,
In laughter's echo, love defined.
By starlit nights and sunlit days,
We stitch our lives in endless ways.

Each tear we shed binds us still tighter,
In darkness found, our sparks grow brighter.
With every challenge, we'll rise above,
For in our hearts, we hold our love.

Vows of old and futures spun,
In every breath, we are as one.
Through shifting tides, we won't be lost,
Together we'll pay the love's sweet cost.

The Architecture of Us

Blueprints drawn on hearts so pure,
In every glance, our spirits stir.
With loving beams and walls of trust,
We build our dreams, a sacred must.

Pillars strong of laughter's sound,
Foundation laid on solid ground.
Windows wide to let in light,
Our love, a beacon warm and bright.

Each room a chapter, stories shared,
In whispered secrets, we are bared.
Through storms and calm, we'll stand so tall,
In this structure, love conquers all.

Gables proud in sunset's gold,
A tale of warmth in every fold.
With time, our walls will wear and age,
Yet still, we write our sacred page.

Together, here's our started plan,
In harmony, we make our stand.
Each brick a moment, each turn a trust,
In the architecture of us.

Mosaics of Affection

Scattered pieces, bright and true,
Colors blend, a vibrant hue.
Each shard reflects a whispered sigh,
In our tapestry, we'll fly high.

Fragments shaped by hands of fate,
Together, building something great.
In laughter's glow, our hearts align,
Each moment shines, a life divine.

Through trials faced and tears we shed,
Love's mosaic, where we've tread.
Bits of joy and times of sorrow,
Crafting dreams for bright tomorrow.

Glimmers dance in shadows cast,
In every piece, a spell is cast.
Collecting memories, near or far,
In this art, our love's a star.

Pieced together, hand in hand,
A beautiful puzzle, wonderfully planned.
Mosaics of affection, bold and bright,
In every corner, pure delight.

Shadows of the Heart

In whispered woods, where shadows play,
Our secrets linger, night and day.
In depths of silence, love takes flight,
Two tender souls embrace the night.

Among the trees, our fears retreat,
In twilight's glow, we feel complete.
The pulsing rhythm of twilight air,
In gentle whispers, we lay bare.

With every heartbeat, shadows grow,
In twilight's embrace, our love will flow.
Through darkened paths, we forge our way,
In shadows, bright, we'll find our stay.

With every step, we dance with time,
In moonlit fields, our hearts will rhyme.
Forever bound through light and dark,
In shadows deep, you are my spark.

Together we'll face the longest night,
With love as armor, hearts so bright.
In the silent echoes, we depart,
In shadows softened, lives impart.

Intricate Weavings

Threads of silver, softly spun,
Patterns dance as shadows run.
Colors blend, a tapestry,
A story whispered, wild and free.

In the loom, the heartbeats meet,
Fingers trace each pulse, each beat.
Dances woven, dreams to hold,
In every stitch, a tale unfolds.

Moments stitched, both near and far,
A fabric rich, like the evening star.
Frayed edges tell of time's embrace,
In every weave, a sacred space.

With patience, art begins to flow,
Through knots and twists, we learn and grow.
Intricate hope in every strand,
Together still, we make our stand.

Each turn, a choice, a path we choose,
In every hue, we spark and fuse.
A world created, soft yet bold,
In intricate weavings, our souls are told.

Harmonies of Handholding

Fingers intertwined, a gentle grace,
In quiet moments, we find our place.
The warmth of touch, a melody sweet,
In every heartbeat, our lives entreat.

A whisper of love, softly shared,
Unspoken words, how much we cared.
With every squeeze, connections grow,
In harmonies bright, our spirits glow.

A dance of palms, a tender sway,
Guiding each other, come what may.
Through trials faced, and joys embraced,
With hands held tight, we've interlaced.

Beneath the stars, we dream anew,
In silence shared, our love rings true.
With every touch, a promise made,
In harmonies found, our fears will fade.

Through life's grand symphony, side by side,
In rhythms of love, we take our stride.
Together we'll stand, forever bold,
In harmonies bright, our story told.

The Framework of Forever

In every frame, a moment caught,
Time stands still in what we've sought.
The pictures tell of laughter, tears,
In every glance, the weight of years.

A canvas stretched, our dreams ignite,
The colors blend, our hopes take flight.
The structure built on trust and care,
In each foundation, memories share.

The walls of time, both thick and thin,
Within these lines, our lives begin.
Through storms weathered and skies so bright,
The framework holds, our love's delight.

With every nail, a vow upheld,
In dreams constructed, our hearts compelled.
Together we stand, through joy and strife,
In this framework of forever, we find our life.

Beyond the frame, horizons vast,
With hands entwined, we're free at last.
In this eternal dance we play,
In the framework of forever, we'll stay.

Lines of Longing

In quiet nights, where silence reigns,
I trace your name on window panes.
A whisper carried on the air,
In every thought, I find you there.

The stars above, they brightly shine,
In constellations, your heart aligns.
Each twinkling light, a wish bestowed,
In lines of longing, our love flowed.

With every heartbeat, distance shrinks,
In dreams we weave, the soul instinct.
The space between, a tender ache,
In lines of longing, love's path we make.

Days turn to months, yet still I yearn,
In memories held, your touch I learn.
Our spirits dance, though far apart,
In lines of longing, I hold your heart.

One day we'll bridge this endless night,
In every dawn, our love ignites.
Until that day, I'll softly sigh,
In lines of longing, our souls will fly.

Fragments of Forever

In a whisper of twilight's grace,
Dreams linger in shadows' embrace.
Soft echoes of laughter remain,
Carved deeply in joy and in pain.

Stars twinkle in the night's soft lace,
Time dances in a fleeting chase.
Moments fold like a fragile leaf,
Each fragment holds a hidden grief.

The heart stitches what time can't mend,
A tapestry we all can depend.
Threads woven in colors of light,
Binding us through the longest night.

In the silence, we find our way,
Guided by memories that sway.
The past and present intertwine,
In fragments that forever shine.

Whispers of love in the cool night air,
Moments etched with tender care.
These fragments, though scattered far,
Reflect the beauty of who we are.

The Poetry of Affinity

Two souls drifting, finding their way,
In the chaos, we choose to stay.
Words spoken in the softest tone,
Building bridges, never alone.

Like rivers merging, paths so clear,
In every laughter, joy and cheer.
Affinity penned in delicate lines,
A dance of hearts that brightly shines.

Shared glances like verses of song,
In this bond, we forever belong.
In each heartbeat, a story unfolds,
A melody of love, silently told.

Finding solace in words profound,
In whispers, a connection is found.
Together we weave a tapestry bright,
The poetry of affinity ignites.

Hand in hand through the cosmic fair,
Moments crafted with utmost care.
Our paths entwined, a beautiful fate,
In the poetry of us, we resonate.

The Art of Embrace

In a world that spins and sways,
Love holds tight through all our days.
A gentle touch, a knowing glance,
In our hearts, a timeless dance.

Arms around, where worries fade,
In your warmth, my fears evade.
Each embrace, a soft retreat,
In silence, our souls meet.

With every hug, a promise made,
In the shadows, love won't trade.
In this art, we paint our love,
Colors bright like stars above.

Time may pass, the world may change,
Yet our bond will never estrange.
Each moment shared, a brush of grace,
In the art of our embrace.

Together we create our space,
A sanctuary where we chase.
In every hold, a story told,
The art of love, forever bold.

Constructions of Kindred Spirits

In laughter's echo, spirits align,
Two hearts converge, a perfect sign.
With every tale and every dream,
We build a bond, stitched at the seam.

Foundations laid in trust and cheer,
Constructing hope when shadows near.
In shared moments, our strength we find,
The beauty of the kindred mind.

Rising high on wings of grace,
Trust and love in every place.
Each brick a memory, safe and clear,
In this fortress, we hold dear.

Together we craft what life can give,
In every moment, learn to live.
The joy we share, a beacon bright,
In constructions of spirits unites.

Through storms and sun, we shall remain,
In laughter, solace, joy, and pain.
With kindred hearts, we'll pave the way,
Creating dreams in every day.

Palettes of Perception

Colors blend in the evening light,
Shadows dance, taking flight.
Each hue tells a tale anew,
A vivid world, a painter's view.

Brush strokes whisper, secrets shared,
In every canvas, dreams declared.
Emotions paint with joyful grace,
A gallery of time and space.

The mind's eye crafts what's felt inside,
Bursting forth, there's nowhere to hide.
Reality bends, as visions entwine,
In every shade, our truths align.

A palette blooms with every heart,
Splashes of life—a work of art.
With open eyes, we draw near,
In this spectrum, nothing to fear.

The Crafting of Companionship

Two hands meet in soft embrace,
Shared laughter fills the empty space.
Moments woven, a tapestry bright,
Together they forge through day and night.

Stories echo in warmth and trust,
Building bridges, a bond robust.
In silence spoken, in glances shared,
A treasure trove of dreams declared.

Through storms and calm, they stand as one,
In the journey of life—never done.
Each step forward, a stride in grace,
In the crafting of home, they find their place.

Through trials faced and joy embraced,
In the heart's ledger, love is traced.
Together they rise, together they stand,
In the dance of time, hand in hand.

Hearts in Harmony

Melodies sing from souls aligned,
In symphonies where hearts combined.
Every note, a gentle sway,
Together they find their way.

Rhythms pulse in the quiet night,
Creating magic, a shared delight.
The music flows, a seamless dream,
In unity, voices gleam.

Chords of laughter, shimmering bright,
Resonate in the soft moonlight.
Harmony thrives where love is found,
In every heartbeat, a joyful sound.

Dancing through life's shifting tide,
Hand in hand, with hearts as guide.
In perfect pitch, they take their stance,
Together they write their beautiful dance.

Threads of Connection

Woven strands of fate entwine,
In every touch, a spark divine.
Invisible ties that pull us close,
In the fabric of life, we chose.

Stitches shared in laughter's grace,
Sewn together in time and space.
Each thread a story, a deeper part,
Embroidered whispers of the heart.

Across the miles, connections grow,
In silent moments, we come to know.
From every tear to every cheer,
The ties we share, forever near.

Patterns unfold, a tapestry bright,
In colors rich, our spirits ignite.
Through every trial, the threads stay strong,
In the quilt of life, where we belong.

The Alchemy of Affection

In whispered tones they share their dreams,
A bond forged in the twilight beams.
With every laugh, a spark ignites,
Transforming shadows into lights.

Through trials faced and laughter shared,
Their hearts entwined, forever paired.
Each moment treasured, a golden thread,
In the tapestry of love they've spread.

With gentle touch, they learn to grow,
In the garden where feelings flow.
An elixir brewed, so sweet and rare,
In the alchemy of love, they bare.

So let the world fade into gray,
For in each other, they find their way.
With every pulse, a rhythm found,
In this dance of love, they're spellbound.

Choreography of Connection

Two souls dancing in twilight's glow,
With every step, their secrets flow.
In sync they move, a rhythm defined,
A ballet of hearts, perfectly lined.

In silence shared, their gaze aligns,
Each heartbeat sings, seamless designs.
Like branches swaying in the breeze,
They twist and turn with graceful ease.

A waltz of trust, in whispers spun,
Two bodies merge, becoming one.
In harmony found, a sweet embrace,
In this choreography, love finds its place.

Though storms may come and shadows play,
They dance beneath, come what may.
With every challenge, they redefine,
The art of love, a dance divine.

The Heart's Compass

In the stillness of the night, they roam,
Each heartbeat marks the way back home.
A compass forged in trust and grace,
Guiding them through time and space.

With every glance, a path unfurls,
Their journey rich with hidden pearls.
Through valleys low and mountains high,
Together they soar, in dreams they fly.

In moments of doubt, the stars align,
Their hearts remind, they are divine.
A gentle nudge, a soft caress,
In love's embrace, they find their rest.

Through winding roads and labyrinths vast,
They navigate the shadows cast.
With every whisper, the truth is found,
The heart's compass, forever bound.

Etching in Eternity

In the canvas of time, they leave their mark,
A tale of love igniting a spark.
With strokes of passion, each moment drawn,
Etched in eternity, never gone.

Like constellations in the midnight sky,
Their love shines bright, forever high.
In every laugh, in every tear,
They carve a legacy, crystal clear.

Through seasons changing, they stand tall,
In the gallery of memories, they enthrall.
With every heartbeat, a story unfolds,
An epic adventure, in love retold.

In the ink of time, their whispers remain,
A timeless bond that conquers pain.
Forever embraced, in love's decree,
They find their peace, eternally free.

The Architecture of Togetherness

First, we lay each brick with care,
Building dreams upon the air.
Windows wide, we let in light,
A refuge found in shared delight.

Columns strong, they reach on high,
Binding hearts as time drifts by.
Together we sketch every plan,
In this space, we understand.

Paths converge within these walls,
Echoes of laughter fill the halls.
Hand in hand, we shape each hour,
In unity, we find our power.

Above, a sky both vast and blue,
Beneath, the roots of me and you.
The architecture we create,
A testament to shared fate.

So raise your voice, let it resound,
In harmony, we stand our ground.
Together, we embrace the dawn,
In this love, we are reborn.

Labyrinth of Longing

In shadows deep, my heart does roam,
Each turn a quest to find a home.
Whispers call from every nook,
In silence, I retrace each look.

Walls of memories wane and rise,
In this maze, truth wears a disguise.
Footsteps echo past the seams,
Chasing fleeting, tangled dreams.

Paths diverge at every glance,
Yearning blooms within the dance.
Searching for a thread to weave,
In longing's grasp, I still believe.

As walls entwine, I feel the sway,
Of hope that guides me on my way.
With every turn, a lesson learned,
In the heart's fire, love is burned.

At last, I reach a sunlit space,
Where longing fades in warm embrace.
The labyrinth, a journey true,
In finding me, I find you.

Threads of Time

In gentle weaves, the moments blend,
Past and future, they transcend.
A tapestry of dusk and dawn,
With every thread, a story drawn.

Colors brush the fabric's face,
Each stitch a whisper, a trace of grace.
Time unravels, yet it binds,
In every heart, its rhythm finds.

We gather threads from days gone by,
Woven memories that never die.
In laughter's hue and sorrow's shade,
The patterns swirl, the fabric made.

Through ages worn, it tells the tale,
Of dreams that soared and hearts that pale.
A guide through storms and sweet reprieve,
A reminder of what we believe.

So hold the threads with tender care,
In every weave, a love we share.
The fabric of our lives entwined,
In threads of time, our souls aligned.

Harmonizing Frequencies

In stillness, find the quiet tone,
Each heartbeat a note of our own.
Waves of sound in perfect blend,
Melodies that twist and bend.

A symphony born from every sigh,
Notes that dance and freely fly.
In laughter's light, our spirits rise,
Harmonies beneath the skies.

Resonance flows through each embrace,
Creating rhythms we can trace.
In every glance, a song unfolds,
In whispered dreams, our music holds.

Together we create the song,
In every moment, we belong.
Tuning hearts to life's sweet beat,
In this harmony, we are complete.

So let the world spin round and round,
In unison, our souls are found.
The frequencies of love remain,
In every chord, our hearts' refrain.

Colors of Comprehension

In hues of thought, the mind unfolds,
Whispers of truth in colors bold.
Each shade a lesson, softly spoke,
A canvas bright where dreams evoke.

Through azure skies, reflections gleam,
Crimson trails of hopes we dream.
Golden rays of wisdom shine,
In every pulse, the stars align.

Emerald echoes through the trees,
Binding hearts with gentle breeze.
Violet visions of what might be,
Artistry of you and me.

Chartreuse paths lead us anew,
In palettes rich, our spirits grew.
Together forging bonds profound,
In colors deep, our truths are found.

So let the spectrum guide our way,
In vibrant tones, we weave and play.
Each step a shade, each breath a tone,
In this mosaic, we are home.

The Mosaic of Emotion

Fragments of laughter, shards of sighs,
Each piece a story, beneath the skies.
Tiles of joy and sorrow blend,
A masterpiece, where feelings mend.

Textures of love stitched with care,
Tender moments dancing in the air.
Crimson heartbeats, sapphire tears,
Constructing tales across the years.

An artist's touch to the canvas bare,
Layering shades with gentle flair.
Glimmers of hope in shadows cast,
In every color, connections last.

Brushstrokes of empathy reveal,
The bonds unbroken, raw and real.
Through every fragment, deep we dive,
In this mosaic, we come alive.

So linger here, in hues we find,
The melodies of heart and mind.
Together we create, explore,
In this mosaic, evermore.

Embracing the Ether

In whispers soft, the ether sings,
A realm of dreams on silent wings.
Where thoughts take flight, and free they roam,
In vast expanse, we find our home.

Nebulae drift in twilight's grasp,
Holding secrets in their clasp.
A cosmic dance of shadows play,
As starlit visions light the way.

Galaxies swirl in tender grace,
A gentle touch, a warm embrace.
In every pulse, the universe knows,
The beauty in how connection flows.

Through ethereal beams, we weave and share,
The essence of love, beyond compare.
In quiet moments, spells we cast,
In timeless realms, our fears surpassed.

So join the dance in this boundless sea,
Of shimmering light and harmony.
Together we rise in ethereal flight,
Embracing the ether, hearts ignite.

Garden of Intertwined Hearts

In fragrant blooms, our stories grow,
A garden rich with love's warm glow.
Petals brushing on the breeze,
Harmonizing, as hearts appease.

Roots enmeshed in earthen grace,
Nurturing dreams in this sacred space.
Vines entwined, a gentle hold,
In whispers shared, our truth unfolds.

Dewdrops glisten in morning light,
Awakening hopes, sparkling bright.
Every flower tells a tale,
In this garden, we shall prevail.

Sun-kissed days and moonlit nights,
Fueling passion, kindling sights.
With every bloom, our spirit thrives,
In this garden, love survives.

So wander here, through paths entwined,
In fragrant whispers, our hearts aligned.
Together we flourish, never apart,
In the garden of intertwined hearts.

Patterns in the Sand

Waves wash the shore with grace,
Leaving marks, a fleeting trace.
Whispers of time in each grain,
Stories written, joy and pain.

Footprints dance and then retreat,
Nature's rhythm, soft and sweet.
Patterns form, then fade away,
Echoes of a brightened day.

Seagulls cry, the sun hangs low,
Breezes carry tales that flow.
Sandcastles rise, then tumble down,
A moment's glory, lost, not found.

Each tide brings a brand new art,
Crafted gently, a tender start.
Life's designs in shifting sands,
A reminder of shifting plans.

In the twilight, shadows play,
Footsteps vanish, night meets day.
Yet in the morning light anew,
Patterns form with skies so blue.

Building Blocks of Belonging

Together we stack our dreams,
Life's foundation built in beams.
Each laugh, a brick, each tear, a stone,
In this space, we are not alone.

Colors combine, like hearts in sync,
Every bond helps us to think.
Walls of trust, they rise and grow,
In the warmth, our spirits glow.

Hand in hand, we shape our fate,
With every choice, we elevate.
A tapestry of voices strong,
In this place, where we belong.

Moments shared, both big and small,
Finding strength in love's strong call.
Together we fortify our ground,
In this harmony, hope is found.

Building bridges, crossing fears,
Through the laughter, through the tears.
Blocks of belonging stood so tall,
In unity, we conquer all.

Sketches of Sweetness

In the garden, colors blend,
Petals whisper, they don't end.
Bright hues dance in morning light,
Nature's canvas, pure delight.

Honey drips from comb so sweet,
Every bite a cherished treat.
Joy unfolds in every taste,
Moments savored, none to waste.

Laughter echoes, soft and clear,
In the warmth, we hold each dear.
Every hug, a gentle trace,
Sketches drawn in love's embrace.

Stars alight with twinkling dreams,
Whispers flow like gentle streams.
Night's embrace, a cozy cloak,
In its warmth, sweet visions smoke.

With each dawn, new hues appear,
Bringing forth the ones we hold near.
Sketches of sweetness, life unfolds,
In these moments, love is bold.

Foundations of Devotion

Roots dug deep in rich, dark soil,
A promise kept through sweat and toil.
Every heartbeat sings a song,
In devotion, we belong.

Bridges built with care and trust,
In this bond, we find what's just.
Hands entwined, we face the storm,
In each other, safe and warm.

Eyes that share a knowing glance,
Together we create our dance.
With each step, we boldly grow,
In this path, our love will flow.

Through trials faced, we stand as one,
Hearts aligned, the day is won.
In our laughter, in our tears,
Foundations strong throughout the years.

Life's great fabric, stitched with care,
In devotion's embrace, we dare.
Together, we'll weather each season,
In this love, we find our reason.

The Map of Us

In every step we take, there lies
A winding path of dreams and sighs.
Together, hand in hand we weave,
A story only we believe.

Beneath the stars, our spirits soar,
Through whispered nights and open doors.
With every heartbeat, maps unfold,
The journey shared, a tale retold.

Through valleys deep and mountains high,
We trace our dreams beneath the sky.
Each twist and turn, a dance of fate,
In every moment, love create.

The compass points where trust remains,
In laughter's joy, in sorrow's chains.
We sketch the future, bright and vast,
Together, here, our shadows cast.

The map of us, a treasure found,
In every silent, sacred sound.
We'll navigate through storms and sun,
Forever joined, we are as one.

Embracing the Infinite

In the stillness of a whisper's flight,
We find the peace in endless night.
Stars align in patterns divine,
Embracing all that intertwines.

Time stretches far in gentle grace,
A canvas wide, an open space.
With each heartbeat, we float and glide,
Infinite, we leave behind the tide.

The universe, a dance of light,
In cosmic arms, we hold on tight.
Every moment, vast and bright,
Guided by the dreams in sight.

Through the echoes of the past,
We chase the moments that forever last.
In the cosmos, our spirits blend,
In this embrace, we transcend.

Together, we are infinite, free,
Boundless as the deep blue sea.
In every breath, in every sigh,
We hold the stars, you and I.

Tapestry of Two

With every thread, our stories blend,
In vibrant hues, on love depend.
Together woven, heart and soul,
A tapestry that makes us whole.

Moments captured, woven tight,
In laughter's weave, in sorrow's night.
Each color tells a tale of bliss,
In the fabric of the love we kiss.

Patterns shift, yet always stay,
Through seasons bright and skies of gray.
We stitch our dreams, both wild and true,
In the tapestry, just me and you.

The knots, they hold our memories dear,
In every stitch, we dry each tear.
Love's design, forever new,
A masterpiece of me and you.

In the loom of life, our hearts entwined,
Creating beauty, ever kind.
Together strong, through all we do,
We are the art, in this tapestry of two.

The Framework of Dreams

In the shadows, dreams do rise,
Built on whispers, hopes, and sighs.
A framework strong to hold the light,
Guiding us through the dark of night.

Each vision forms a sturdy beam,
With every plan, we chase the dream.
In unity, our hopes unite,
Constructing futures, bold and bright.

Through trials faced, the walls we build,
A space where passion is fulfilled.
In every corner, love takes form,
Creating hearts a cherished norm.

Together crafting, brick by brick,
In this framework, time moves quick.
With every heartbeat, stronger we stand,
Dreams entwined, hand in hand.

In the architecture of our fate,
We carve the paths that make us great.
In every dream, a life's regime,
We find our truth in this grand theme.

The Symphony of Our Hearts

In shadows soft, our whispers blend,
Notes of love that never end.
A melody that time can't break,
Together, we awake.

With every beat, our spirits dance,
A rhythm born from sweet romance.
Hands entwined, we grasp the sound,
In our embrace, we're truly found.

Like autumn leaves in golden flight,
Our hearts create a wondrous sight.
A song of dreams, forever true,
The symphony of me and you.

Through stormy nights and sunny days,
Our hearts compose a timeless praise.
The universe, our stage so vast,
In harmony, our love holds fast.

For every note, a story told,
In symphony, we grow bold.
Together in this dance we share,
Our hearts, a song beyond compare.

A Voyage of Affection

Across the waves, our hearts set sail,
In winds of love, we shall prevail.
With each new tide, our spirits rise,
Together carved across the skies.

In harbors calm, we find our peace,
Where troubles fade, and sorrows cease.
With every glance, my compass turns,
For you, my heart forever yearns.

Each shoreside kiss, a treasure found,
In depths of love, and joy unbound.
No storm can sway our steadfast hearts,
In this great voyage, love imparts.

With sails unfurling, hope takes flight,
Guided by stars that shine so bright.
Together we traverse this sea,
In waves of affection, wild and free.

So hand in hand, we brave the tide,
In every ebb, our dreams reside.
A journey grand, forever lush,
In love's embrace, we feel the rush.

The Signature of Souls

In silence deep, our spirits meet,
A bond unbroken, pure and sweet.
With every glance, a truth unfolds,
A story shared, forever told.

Like brush strokes on a canvas wide,
Our souls converse, with hearts as guide.
In every laugh, a spark ignites,
Illuminating our darkest nights.

With ink of dreams, our fates are penned,
In the library of time, we transcend.
No words are needed, only feels,
In the tapestry of love, it heals.

The signature, a mark divine,
Two souls entangled, yours and mine.
In every heartbeat, we convey,
An artful dance in love's ballet.

Together we write a timeless tale,
In every storm, our love won't pale.
With passion's flare, and kindness' grace,
The signature of souls, our place.

Bridging Distances

Across the miles, our hearts align,
In whispered dreams, your hand in mine.
Though far apart, we feel the pull,
Our love, a bond that's beautiful.

In twilight's glow, soft shadows cast,
Each moment cherished, moments past.
We build a bridge with every sigh,
In love's embrace, it will rely.

Through every storm, we share the pain,
In laughter sweet, our hearts remain.
No distance great, no walls can rise,
Our love will soar, like summer skies.

With every sunrise, hope ignites,
A promise kept through endless nights.
For in our hearts, the truth is clear,
Love conquers all, and draws us near.

So here's to us, a love so vast,
In every memory, shadows cast.
Together we'll weave our futures bright,
Through bridges built in love's pure light.

The Corners of Compassion

In shadows cast by silent tears,
We find the warmth that draws us near.
A gentle hand to lift the weight,
Compassion blooms, defying fate.

Where heartbeats whisper, kindness grows,
Each shared burden softly flows.
In every smile, a spark ignites,
Uniting souls on lonely nights.

We tread the paths of grace and light,
Embracing dreams that take to flight.
Together, we can mend the seams,
Woven tightly, stitched with dreams.

Through trials faced, our spirits soar,
In unity, we are much more.
In corners where our fears reside,
Compassion's glow, our timeless guide.

So let us stand, hand in hand,
And craft a world, so bright and grand.
For in this dance of hearts so bold,
Compassion's tale forever told.

Echoes Beneath Stars

Beneath the veil of night so deep,
The whispers of the cosmos sweep.
Each echo tells a timeless tale,
Of dreams that soar, of hearts that sail.

Stars like lanterns in the dark,
Guiding wanderers with their spark.
In quiet moments, wishes soar,
As echoes call from distant shores.

The moonlight bathes the world in gold,
As secrets of the night unfold.
Thoughts drift lightly on midnight air,
In echoes, we find all we share.

With every twinkle, stories blend,
The universe, a timeless friend.
In silence, we unite our minds,
While in the stars, our peace we find.

So let us stargaze, hand in hand,
And forge our dreams upon this land.
In echoes of the night so vast,
We find our future, united, steadfast.

The Frame of Friendship

In laughter's light, friendships grow strong,
A tapestry stitched with a song.
In moments shared, we dance with grace,
Creating memories, time can't erase.

With open hearts, we bridge the space,
Between our dreams, a warm embrace.
In trials faced, we stand as one,
Together shining like the sun.

Through storms that come and shadows fall,
Friendship's warmth will lead us all.
In every challenge, hand in hand,
We carve our path upon the sand.

With trust as paint and laughter's hue,
We frame our lives in colors true.
In every heartbeat, every sigh,
Our bond holds firm, it will not die.

So raise a glass to friendships dear,
For in their light, we conquer fear.
In every chapter, every blend,
We flourish in the frame of friends.

A Journey of Warmth

With every step, the road unfolds,
A journey rich, its tale retold.
Through winding paths and valleys low,
The warmth we share will surely grow.

In sunlit days and rainy nights,
We find the spark that lights our sights.
Through laughter bright and shared delight,
Our hearts ignite, the world feels right.

As seasons change and winds may shift,
A journey's gold is love's true gift.
With arms wide open, we take flight,
Through every dawn, we chase the light.

Together, facing what may come,
In unity, we overcome.
With every heartbeat, every glance,
A journey born of love's sweet dance.

So hand in hand, we walk our way,
A flame of warmth that will not sway.
In every step, we'll find our home,
A journey made, wherever we roam.

Threads of Tenderness

In quiet whispers, hearts unfold,
Stitched together, love untold.
Softened edges, gentle hue,
Binding souls with love so true.

Each thread a promise, softly spun,
Woven tightly, two as one.
In warmth we find our refuge here,
Threads of tenderness, held so dear.

Through storms that rage and seasons change,
Our tapestry will not estrange.
With every stitch, our dream ignites,
Guiding us through darkest nights.

In laughter shared and silence sweet,
Life's vibrant patterns, heartbeats meet.
Together we dance, a gentle sway,
In threads of tenderness, we find our way.

With colors bold, we paint our scene,
Unravel fears, let love convene.
The fabric of our lives, entwined,
A legacy of hearts defined.

A Symphony of Souls

In the quiet, music wakes,
Each note a heartbeat, life it makes.
A dance of spirits, soft and bright,
A symphony that takes its flight.

In harmony, we find our path,
United voices, love's sweet math.
With every chord, a bond released,
In this embrace, our fears are ceased.

Together we weave our melodies,
Through whispered dreams and gentle pleas.
Resounding waves of joy and peace,
In every note, our hearts increase.

In moments shared, like strings we play,
Creating magic, night and day.
The echoes linger, sweet and pure,
A symphony of souls, we endure.

Through life's crescendo, we will stand,
In every beat, we understand.
A rhythm formed in love's embrace,
A symphony that time can't erase.

Heartfelt Designs

In the fabric of our dreams,
Patterns form in flowing seams.
Each stitch reflects the love we bind,
Heartfelt designs, uniquely kind.

With colors bright and shades of grace,
We craft our home, a sacred space.
Through trials faced, each challenge met,
Our heartfelt designs, no regret.

Layered stories, rich and vast,
In every thread, our voices cast.
Together we navigate and rise,
In heartfelt designs, love never dies.

A canvas spread beneath our hands,
We sketch our dreams in shifting sands.
Embracing changes, all we find,
In heartfelt designs, forever intertwined.

Embroidered hopes and laughter shared,
In every fold, a love declared.
With each new dawn, we start anew,
Creating patterns made for two.

The Codex of Companionship

In the library of our lives,
Written tales where friendship thrives.
Each page a memory, crisp and clear,
The codex whispers, 'I am here.'

Through laughter, tears, we pen our fate,
In silent moments, love holds weight.
Every chapter, a story spun,
In the codex, we are one.

Bound with trust like finest gold,
Our secrets shared, our hearts unfold.
In every turn, the lessons learned,
The codex of companionship, we yearned.

With every word, a promise made,
A timeless bond that won't soon fade.
Through trials faced, our hopes can soar,
In the codex, we choose to explore.

Hand in hand, let's write once more,
New adventures at each page's core.
A journey shared, we relish deep,
The codex of companionship we keep.

Heartstrings Unraveled

In the twilight glow, we stand,
Fingers touching, soft and warm,
Whispers shared, a bond so grand,
Love's sweet scent, a gentle charm.

Threads of fate entwined so tight,
Pulling softly, heart by heart,
In your eyes, I see the light,
A masterpiece, a work of art.

Time may fray the edges near,
Yet our pulse remains the same,
With every joy, and every tear,
We'll forever play this game.

Every laugh and every sigh,
Stitching moments, day by day,
Through the storms, we'll never cry,
In your arms, I wish to stay.

As the world around us spins,
We'll find solace in the chase,
Bound by love that never thins,
You and I, in our own space.

The Architecture of Affection

Crafted walls of trust we build,
Each brick laid with tender care,
In our hearts, a love fulfilled,
A sanctuary, always there.

Windows wide, let sunlight pour,
Illuminating paths we tread,
In this place, our spirits soar,
Every tear and joy we've shed.

Blueprints sketched in laughter's song,
Echo in the halls we roam,
In our haven, we belong,
Together we've created home.

Every corner holds a dream,
Each foundation steady, strong,
In our world, we are a team,
Hand in hand, we both belong.

When the night begins to fall,
With warmth, we cocoon our hearts,
In this structure, love's enthrall,
An architecture that never parts.

Maps of Intimacy

In the valleys of your gaze,
I trace the lines that lead to you,
Every moment, a soft blaze,
In our map, the journey's true.

Rivers flow, emotions deep,
Crossing bridges built from trust,
In the silence, secrets keep,
A roadmap drawn, a must.

Through the storms, we'll find our way,
With compass points aligned as one,
Underneath the moon's soft sway,
Every mile a race well run.

Each turn taken brings us near,
Navigating love's unknown,
In your heart, I have no fear,
With each step, love has grown.

As we chart this life anew,
Hand in hand, through thick and thin,
With every path that leads us through,
Maps of love will always win.

The Framework of Us

In the quiet of the night,
We build a frame that holds our dreams,
With each heartbeat, pure delight,
Together, nothing's as it seems.

Caught in laughter, woven tight,
Every thread a silent vow,
In the chaos, we find light,
United in the here and now.

Nails of trust, glue of grace,
Crafting moments, day by day,
In this intricate embrace,
Love's reflection guides our way.

Every twist and every turn,
Strengthening this sacred bond,
In our hearts, a fire burns,
Through the ages, we respond.

In the framework built for two,
Love constructs what life bestows,
Through all trials, we'll break through,
Hand in hand, forever flows.

The Design of Dreams

In shadows cast by moonlit beams,
Soft whispers spark a world of dreams.
A canvas bright, where wishes fly,
In the silent night, they never die.

Starlit paths lead souls astray,
Through the realms where night meets day.
Colors swirl, and visions gleam,
Each heartbeat sings of a timeless dream.

The mind's eye paints with hues so rare,
Each thought a thread, woven with care.
Patterns dance in vibrant streams,
As the heart unravels its tapestry of dreams.

In the cradle of night, hope ignites,
Guiding the way to newfound heights.
Chasing shadows, we become the light,
In the design of dreams, we take flight.

Patterns Woven in Time

Threads of gold in the fabric fine,
Whisper tales in every line.
Moments captured, never fade,
In patterns woven, memories laid.

Time's gentle hands caress each seam,
Stitching together the heart's soft dream.
Echoes linger in every fold,
Stories cherished, waiting to be told.

Seasons change, yet we remain,
Bound by love, joy, and pain.
Each breath a note in the grand design,
Of patterns woven in sacred time.

Glimmers of hope in the darkest night,
Guiding us home, illuminating light.
In every heartbeat, our spirits chime,
As we dance to the rhythm of time.

The Pulse of Connection

In every smile, a spark ignites,
The pulse of connection, a shared light.
Hands reach out, hearts intertwine,
In silent understandings, love does shine.

Words unspoken, yet deeply felt,
In every glance, the heart does melt.
Bridges built from soul to soul,
In this dance, we find our whole.

Through laughter and tears, we find our way,
The pulse of connection, come what may.
An unseen thread that binds us tight,
In the tapestry of life, love takes flight.

Together we walk, through storms we dare,
Knowing that always, someone will care.
In the gentle rhythm, we truly believe,
In the pulse of connection, we weave and receive.

Threads of Destiny

In the loom of fate, we find our path,
Threads of destiny, woven by math.
Each encounter, a stitch in time,
Creating patterns, a rhythm, a rhyme.

Whispers of choices echo in the night,
Guiding us gently, showing the light.
With every move, a chance we create,
In the journey of life, we navigate fate.

Hearts bound together by invisible ties,
In the dance of dreams, where hope ne'er dies.
As the tapestry grows, we see it unfold,
The stories of life, in colors so bold.

Through trials and joys, we find our way,
With threads of destiny, come what may.
In the fabric of time, we weave and spin,
Finding our place, as the journey begins.

Sculpted in Sentiment

In shadows carved, the heart does rest,
Whispers linger, secrets confessed.
Each moment molds a tender trace,
A memory wrapped in soft embrace.

Echoes dance in twilight's glow,
Emotions rise, like tides that flow.
With every sigh, with every tear,
Love's sculptor moves, forever near.

Interlaced Journeys

Winding paths that cross and weave,
In the tapestry, we believe.
Every step, a story true,
Crafted by me, designed by you.

Footprints linger on golden sands,
Holding dreams in gentle hands.
Through tangled trees and starlit skies,
Together we soar, where wisdom lies.

Navigating by Starlight

Beneath a blanket of endless night,
Stars above guide us in their light.
With every wish, a path unfolds,
In cosmic tales that time beholds.

Each twinkle tells of journeys past,
Of love's embrace that holds us fast.
In quiet moments, we find our way,
Navigating dreams until the day.

The Fabric of Us

Threads entwined, our lives connect,
In vibrant hues, respect reflects.
Woven stories tell our truth,
In fabric soft, we find our youth.

With every stitch, a bond grows strong,
In laughter shared, we both belong.
Through dusk and dawn, our hearts align,
Crafting a love that feels divine.

The Texture of Together

In the quiet of the night,
Hands entwined, a gentle fight.
Whispers blend in soft embrace,
Creating warmth in this shared space.

Laughter echoes through the room,
Chasing shadows, dispelling gloom.
Every moment, a tender thread,
Woven tightly, where love is shed.

Hearts beat in a rhythmic dance,
Finding meaning in each glance.
Together we build, brick by brick,
A tapestry with every click.

In the storms, we stand as one,
Facing challenges till they're done.
Through the storms and through the calm,
Together we find our balm.

As the years weave memories bright,
With every dawn, we draw in light.
Though time may fade, we will remain,
In the texture where love is lain.

Blueprints of Belonging

In the heart of a bustling place,
We sketch our dreams with quiet grace.
Lines and colors, pathways bright,
In our souls, we find our light.

Every face tells a unique tale,
As we journey, we set sail.
Connecting dots of different hues,
Crafting bonds that will not lose.

Through laughter shared and tears we shed,
In every word, all needs are fed.
Together we form a sturdy frame,
In this house of love, we claim.

Hand in hand, we break the mold,
Sharing stories, bravely bold.
In the chaos, we find our song,
In this place, we all belong.

As we turn the pages new,
Our blueprints draw a vibrant view.
In the architecture of our days,
Together we'll set hearts ablaze.

Synergy of Souls

In the dance of fate and chance,
Two souls meet, sparked by romance.
Echoes of a past long gone,
In this union, hope is drawn.

Energy flows like a gentle stream,
Filling spaces, igniting a dream.
With every heartbeat, we align,
Creating moments truly divine.

In the laughter, in quiet sighs,
We find truth in each other's eyes.
A fusion of hearts, a radiant glow,
In this synergy, love will grow.

Through the valleys and the peaks,
In our stillness, the universe speaks.
Together, we paint the skies above,
In the rhythm of our shared love.

As stars convene in the midnight blue,
Each glance exchanged feels so true.
In our synergy, we find a way,
To light the path of each new day.

Writing Our Story

With every word, we craft a tale,
Ink and heart, in love we sail.
Pages worn from stories shared,
In this journey, we have fared.

Characters born from laughter's grace,
Setting scenes in time and space.
Through joy and pain, we carve our lines,
In the margins, love still shines.

Each chapter ends, yet not goodbye,
For in our hearts, we'll always fly.
Plot twists come, but never stray,
Together we'll find another way.

With hope as our guiding star,
We'll write the verses near and far.
Turning pages, with every seam,
In our story, forever dream.

As the final lines approach the end,
With every heartbeat, love we send.
In this book, we've forged our name,
Writing our story, never the same.

Interwoven Paths

In quiet corners, fate will meet,
Two lives connected, a dance discreet.
Footsteps echo on winding trails,
Together through winds and gentle gales.

Roots entwined where shadows dwell,
Stories whispered, a timeless spell.
Paths that twist with every turn,
A bond that grows, a hearth's warm burn.

Through laughter shared and sorrows faced,
In moments fleeting, love is laced.
Among the stars, our dreams take flight,
Interwoven paths in the soft moonlight.

Each step forward, a memory made,
In every glance, a promise laid.
Together we forge a brighter way,
As dawn breaks new at the end of day.

In the tapestry of life we weave,
Threads of hope that we believe.
Interwoven paths that fate has spun,
Two hearts in rhythm, forever one.

Sketching Serendipity

A chance encounter, a fleeting glance,
In crowded rooms, we find our dance.
With every smile, the colors blend,
Sketching memories we won't pretend.

With gentle strokes, the moments flow,
A masterpiece born in the afterglow.
Invisible threads pull us near,
In serendipity, there's nothing to fear.

Lines may waver, and shadows cross,
But in this art, there's never loss.
Each heartbeat sketches a brand-new view,
As stories intertwine in every hue.

Brushes dipped in laughter and tears,
Creating dreams that shatter fears.
In the gallery of chance we dwell,
Sketching serendipity, a tale to tell.

With every twist, the canvas grows,
In every pause, the wonder shows.
Together we paint, our spirits free,
In a world of chance, just you and me.

Spaces Between Beats

In silences shared, our hearts align,
In the spaces where moments entwine.
A heartbeat echoes, soft and slow,
In every pause, our feelings grow.

Between the notes, a symphony plays,
Unspoken words in gentle ways.
Each glance lingers, a soft caress,
In the quiet, we find our rest.

The tempo shifts with each soft sigh,
In the empty spaces, we learn to fly.
Rhythms dance in tender embrace,
In sacred stillness, we find our place.

Time may wander like a soft breeze,
But here in the silence, we find our ease.
Tangled together in life's sweet song,
In every space where we belong.

Between the beats, the world fades away,
In the harmony, forever we'll stay.
Together we breathe in perfect time,
In the spaces between, our souls will rhyme.

Creating our Connection

Two hearts collide in a world so vast,
From whispered dreams, a bond is cast.
With every word, we craft the light,
Creating our connection, pure and bright.

In gardens grown from tender care,
We find a haven, a space to share.
With roots that dig in the depths below,
Together we flourish, together we grow.

Threads of laughter weave through the day,
In shadows of doubt, we find our way.
Building bridges with each tender touch,
In the tapestry of love, we learn so much.

A symphony of moments, soft and sweet,
In every heartbeat, our souls compete.
Creating our connection, a dance divine,
In this world of chaos, a love that shines.

Forever entwined in the best of times,
In moonlit dreams and soft chimes.
Together we face whatever's sent,
Creating our connection, our hearts' intent.

The Symphony of Souls

In the quiet night, dreams take flight,
Whispering secrets, hearts ignite.
Notes of laughter, tears in tune,
A melody shared beneath the moon.

Harmony flows, each soul aligned,
Connecting rhythms, love intertwined.
With every heartbeat, a song unfolds,
In this symphony, our story told.

Strings of the past, woven with care,
Echo through time, memories rare.
A chorus of voices, strong and free,
Together we create our symphony.

In the dance of life, we sway and spin,
Inviting others, let the music in.
With every note, a bond we form,
In the symphony, we are reborn.

So let us sing, let our spirits soar,
In this grand concert, forevermore.
A celebration of souls, hand in hand,
The symphony of life, a timeless band.

Patterns of Passion

In every heartbeat, a pattern grows,
Colors of longing, the passion flows.
Strokes of desire paint the sky,
A tapestry woven, where dreams lie.

Textures of hope, brushed with fear,
Each moment speaks, crystal clear.
Layers of love, both thick and thin,
A dance of flames, where we begin.

Echoes of laughter, shadows of tears,
Entwined together through fleeting years.
With every whisper, a tale we tell,
In patterns of passion, we've learned to dwell.

Kaleidoscope visions of what is true,
In vibrant hues, I see you too.
Each day a canvas, fresh and bright,
Framing the wonder, igniting the night.

So let us capture the moments we share,
In patterns of passion, a love laid bare.
Together we sketch, together we dream,
In this world of colors, we forever gleam.

Building Bridges of Belonging

Across the waters, we stretch our hands,
Bridging the gaps, uniting our lands.
With beams of kindness, we pave the way,
For hearts to gather, for souls to play.

Each plank a story, each nail a bond,
In the warmth of connection, we grow fond.
Together we walk on this bridge of trust,
Finding our peace, as we must.

The whispers of strangers, now friends we find,
In the spaces between, our hearts unlined.
Through storms and sunshine, we hold our ground,
In the framework of love, we're tightly bound.

To build is to hope, to reach for the stars,
No matter the distance, no matter the scars.
With every step taken, with every embrace,
We nurture the beauty of a shared place.

So let's raise our voices, let our laughter ring,
In the bridge of belonging, together we sing.
Creating a haven where all feel free,
Building a future, just you and me.

The Canvas of Companionship

On a blank canvas, we start anew,
Brushstrokes of friendship, vibrant hue.
Each color a story, a smile, a tear,
In the canvas of life, you're always near.

Together we wander through shadow and light,
Creating our masterpiece, day and night.
With laughter as paint and love as our guide,
In this canvas of companionship, we confide.

The gentle strokes of kindness shine bright,
In every corner, hope takes flight.
We layer our dreams, building them high,
With each passing moment, our spirits fly.

Textures of trust, intertwined fate,
In this quiet refuge, we both create.
Side by side, as artists, we grow,
Painting a world where love can flow.

So here we stand, brush in hand,
In the canvas of companionship, we take a stand.
With every heartbeat, a color we choose,
Together we'll paint, together we'll lose.

Blueprinted Hearts

In a world of lines and curves,
We sketch our dreams in stars,
With every heartbeat, we form,
Blueprints of who we are.

Together we draft our fate,
Building bridges, not just walls,
In the architecture of love,
Each moment captured, enthralls.

Every whisper, a soft design,
Every glance, a perfect space,
In the canvas of our souls,
We find our sacred place.

With hopes and fears intertwined,
We construct a realm so bright,
Where every flaw holds beauty,
In the shadows, shines the light.

Our hearts are maps of journeys,
Each scar a story told,
In this blueprint of existence,
Love remains, fierce and bold.

Choreography of Togetherness

In the dance of soft whispers,
We move in rhythm, so fine,
With every step, a promise,
In this waltz, your hand in mine.

The world fades in our echoes,
As we pirouette through the night,
With laughter as our melody,
Together, we set hearts alight.

In the ballroom of our dreams,
Steps crafted by trust and grace,
Each twirl writes our story,
In this enchanted space.

The tempo quickens, we leap,
A cascade of joy in the air,
In the choreography of souls,
A symphony we both share.

As the music gently swells,
We unite in a final stance,
In this dance of forever,
Our hearts forever in trance.

The Structure of Yearning

In the silence of the night,
A longing fills the void,
Each breath a testament,
Of dreams yet to be enjoyed.

We build our hopes like towers,
Rising high above the pain,
Each brick, a piece of longing,
In the structure of our gain.

The walls echo with whispers,
Of desires softly spoken,
In each crevice of our hearts,
Lie promises unbroken.

With blueprints drawn by starlight,
We sketch a future bright,
In the shadows of our wishes,
Love will always find its light.

The foundation strong beneath us,
Together, we will stand tall,
In the structure of our yearning,
We've built a world for all.

Cartography of the Heart

With every heartbeat charted,
We navigate uncharted seas,
Mapping out our paths in love,
Amongst the rustling trees.

Each memory a compass,
Guiding us through stormy nights,
In the cartography of longing,
We find our way with lights.

Oceans rise and valleys fall,
Yet our map remains so true,
In the landscape of connection,
It is me and it is you.

We traverse through each shadow,
Finding joy in every turn,
In this journey of the heart,
A flame within us burns.

As we explore this vast terrain,
Together, we take flight,
In the cartography of our souls,
Love guides us through the night.

Milton Keynes UK
Ingram Content Group UK Ltd.
UKHW020744051024
449151UK00011B/418

9 789916 893265